Eternal Joy in Eternity

notionpress.com

ETERNAL JOY
in
ETERNITY

C.B. PAUL CHELLAKUMAR

notionpress
.com

Notion Press

Old No. 38, New No. 6

McNichols Road, Chetpet

Chennai - 600 031

First Published by Notion Press 2016

ISBN 978-93-5206-634-6

To my wife, Grace, who shared my pain of sickness through several sleepless nights.

"For thus saith the high and lofty One that inhabiteth eternity, - Whose name is Holy."

Is 57:15

Contents

Foreword

The mystery of Christianity for those that believe the truths of the Gospel is that the truth has to be lived out 'by faith' in each of our lives. The Gospel is both corporate and individual in nature. The Apostle Paul describes this as "the life I now live in the flesh"—Galatians 2:20. One of the aspects of that life is the certainty of death, unless, of course, the Lord returns in our lifetime. For Christians, death needs to be understood in the context of God's Word, with the Holy Spirit guiding and teaching us on an individual basis. The sin that was perpetrated in the Garden of Eden left a legacy of both spiritual death (separation from the Holy God) and physical death, both of which were overcome by Jesus as evidenced by His death and subsequent resurrection.

Dr. Paul Chellakumar has delivered, from his own experiences, a study into the subject of death. His Biblical research and the testimony of his own experience combine to challenge each of us to gaze at this mystery. A mystery that will be understood by each of us at the end of the time span that the Lord has granted to us on this earth He created. May you enjoy, be challenged, and be encouraged by this book.

I encourage you to meditate on the Word and discover the wonderful truths that are in store for each of us who trust and believe in Jesus our Saviour.

To God be the glory.

Rev. Dr. E. Steve Griffiths

Senior Presbyter and Faculty

Adelaide, South Australia

Generic Views on Eternity

The following are the opinions of people from various walks of life on 'Eternity':

Eternity is the time we will be with our Lord after the judgement. Every believer looks forward to this time with longing.

Mrs. Revathy Bonns, School Principal

Holy God's ultimate desire is to restore His image in human through the blood of Jesus and make the cleansed souls be with them forever in eternity.

Dharmaraj, Advocate

Other than for God and nature, eternity is not a blessing but a curse. Everything should have an end.

Monica Rajesh, Advocate

Eternity—people generally think it is everlasting. Actually it is for things with no beginning. Anything that has a beginning will end. Science one day will prove there is nothing eternal except this book.

A.S. Krishnnan, Sr. Marketing Consultant

Eternity is a state of everlasting existence without any end that generally finds place in fantasy world and not in to-day's life.

Rajeni Ramadoss, Advocate

Eternity is without end, or forever. Heaven is meant for happiness and joy for eternity, while hell is meant for those missing the eternity.

Reymond, Retd Bank Officer

Eternity is a place prepared for me to spend my eternity with my heavenly Father, Who paid the price and redeemed me from my sins. It is going to be my permanent place. The original plan of God will be fulfilled there.

Mrs. Eva, Secretary

If eternity truly exists, then, by definition, we have forever to think about it. Right now, I would rather just focus on the moment at hand.

Raveena Joseph, Journalist

Eternity is the original place and pattern of life planned, designed by Jehovah Elshaddai for mankind, a place of love, peace and joy with God's presence in fullness.

Nirmala Savarirayan, Sr.Trainer

Eternity is real. I believe that the moment we die in earth, we will wake up in another place that becomes eternal to us. This place is heaven for some and hell for others—a reward for the quality relationship we enjoyed with God when we were in earth. Jehovah is the eternity that He is beyond the dimension of time.

Arjun Joseph, College Administrator

Anything whose parameters are not determined by time belongs to eternity. Thus, God, who is spirit and the human soul and mind, whose origin and end are beyond the constraints of time, belong to the realm of eternity. In that sense God is alive, but He does not exist. So also the Human exists, only as longs as the person has a body. After the body perishes, he/she lives but does not exist.

Dr. Arun Gopal, Retd. Presbyter

Eternity implies that which is present at the end, and remains thus forever. However, as every Ending must have a beginning Eternity starts now. It never ends; we do in so far as subjective tracting is concerned.

Dr. Henry L.N. Anderson, University Chancellor

Eternity is truth, Truth is Word of God, He is the Word, Himself Jesus Christ.

Pastor Churchil

Straight is the gate, and narrow is the way, which leadeth unto eternity and a few there be that find it.

Bro. Mohanraj, Evangelist

A person who strongly believes in God knows that God will reward him in the eternal life and that would be the real success. True justice becomes apparent by believing in life after death—the eternity.

Rafiq Salahudeen, Educational Consultant

The journey that we take with God on earth, is the miracle one makes, and through him we see forever, and achieve Eternity.

Gift Anderson, Director

Campus Abroad

Eternity is to be with God—that is why Apostle Paul says to die is a gain for him.

Joseph Jebakumar, Retd Accounts Officer

My quest for Truth and to be closer with God was not available in Himalayas but with Jesus Christ Who Himself is Truth and Way, leading to Eternity. Trust the Bible and find out what happens after death. Truth will set you free.

Mrs. Rehna Kant & Mr. Anil Kant, Popular Singers

I believe in eternity. There is no way anyone could escape eternity. According to me eternity is eternal joy of salvation through Jesus Christ who will be waiting to receive me at the, the other end as Bible says "yea though I walk through the valley of shadow of death I will fear no evil: for thou art with me; thy rod and thy staff they comfort me."

Grace Christobel

We must learn to live in time and eternity simultaneously.

Welsh Preacher

Life is eternal. We have stopped for a moment to encounter each other, to meet, to live, to share. It is precious moment. It is a little parenthesis in eternity.

Deepak Chopra, The Seven Spiritual Laws of Success

Preface

Dear Reader,

Everyone dies. Why, then, do so many fear death? Why is death portrayed as something dark and gloomy? This fear is as old as human life, as long and as widespread as human life. Some people do their utmost to avoid the subject of death, and any mention of 'death' is stigmatised as 'morbid'. "Death is depicted as a master who enslaves—that horrifies us. With all our medical skills we cannot stop death, nor will we able to master, by human achievement, this fatal visitor," said Wayne Jackson. "The fear of death never left me," said William Cory, the poet. However, the Bible says that those who die in Christ shall be blessed henceforth (Rev 14:13).

Every death we come across in our lives is only a reminder that no one is exempted from this final part of life on earth. It is not only a reminder but also a warning that we should set our lives right to avail salvation and follow our Lord Jesus Christ. When an angiogram confirmed a few blocks in my arteries and I was asked to go for angioplasty, fear engulfed me—not for leaving this world but for leaving behind my loved ones and many matters unsettled. In addition to natural fear, satan created within me some doubts and anxieties as to what would happen to my family after my departure. At this juncture, God reminded me that I could do nothing on my own without His help, either for the present or for the future as in the past (Eccl 3:15), and reminded me how I had criticised my father during such a situation when he was in his 80s. This reminder from the Lord prompted me to write this book. I am grateful for the purpose of God, having allowed me to go through this experience, so that I was able to understand what the Psalmist said in Psalm 23:4.

Adam and Eve brought death to the world by their disobedience to God, and were punished with 'death' (Gen 3:19). His clear warning, given earlier to Adam (Gen 2:17), was ignored—as confirmed in Eccl 3:20, and vouched by Psalmist Maschil in 89:48. However, death will be a pleasant and welcome phase for those walking in uprightness, leading them to peace (Is 57:2).

I look upon the Holy Spirit to give me His guidance in this project and I pray to God and wish that by the time you complete reading this book, you would be relieved from the fear of death and be prepared to receive our Lord at any time. The entire subject is covered only through Biblical verses and each verse is supported mostly with another verse of reference, so that you would understand and accept them with all authenticity and faith, and share them with other souls. May God give you His Spirit-filled knowledge to understand and consider everything and every situation in the light of His Word.

Jesus said, "Verily, verily, I say unto thee, except a man be born of water and of the Spirit, he cannot enter into the kingdom of God." The mission of death is to lead us to the Lord, according to our relationship with Him. We need not be anxious much about the nature of death, which means no more than closing our eyes for good on this earth and opening them in heaven in the presence of our Lord. Please go through the entire content not with your own knowledge or understanding but with the help of the Holy Spirit Who only enabled me, to finish this at His appointed time.

With a grateful heart to my Saviour.

C.B. Paul Chellakumar

Birth of Death

"Then shall the dust return to earth as it was; and the Spirit shall return unto God Who gave it."

Eccl 12:7

Birth of Death

For dust thou art and unto dust shall thou return. Gen 3:19.

Disobedience to God's commandments brought death to the world. Yet the first man lived for 930 years (Gen 5:5). Our body is dust and it belongs to dust through death.

For in the day that thou shall surely die. Gen 2:17.

Man was warned that he shall surely die on the day he eats the forbidden fruit—but Adam lived for 930 years, and did not die on the same day that he ate the fruit. This confirms that God's warning was not meant for physical death but for the blessings of the Lord, whereby the first fear got into Adam and he hid himself from the Lord.

Therefore, just as through one man sin entered the world and death by sin and so death spread over to all men, because all sinned. Rom 5:12.

Sin of disobedience brought death to the world, passed upon all men for all have sinned.

Nevertheless death reigned from Adam to Moses even…over those who had not sinned. Rom 5:14.

Death ruled even over those who have not sinned, but they received an abundance of grace and the gift of righteousness to rule with Jesus Christ.

Those who practice such (all unrighteousness) things are worthy of death. Rom. 1:32.

Those who have the knowledge of the judgements of God for unrighteousness, and yet continue with pleasure to be unrighteous deserve death.

The sorrow of the world produces death. II Cor 7:10.

Many sorrows shall be meant for wicked; but he that trusts in the Lord shall be compassed with His mercy (Ps:32:10).

According to Apostle Paul, the sorrow of the world leads to death, but godly sorrows leads to salvation.

The righteous perishes…

Merciful men are taken away…evil to come. Is 57:1.

Even the righteous and merciful men are not exempted from death. But the difference is that the righteous shall enter into peace subject to their salvation after their death.

Was it not with those who sinned, whose corpses fell in the wilderness? Heb 3:17.

Unto whom I sware in my wrath that they should not enter into my rest asks the Psalmist (95:11) Heb 3:18.

Only those who sinned in wilderness were made to die for their sins.

The Lord has not forsaken His kindness to the living and the dead. Ruth 2:20.

The kindness and mercy of the Lord are guaranteed to the living as well as to the dead in Christ. The Lord was kind and merciful to Ruth, who has been described as the gentle bride of Christ.

And how does a wise man die? Eccl 2:16.

Whether you are wise or unwise, you will have to die one day. The wisest king asks himself, "As it happens to the fool, so it happens to the WISE, so it happens even to me—and why was I then more wise?" Remember, death is meant for everyone, irrespective of one's status.

For whoever desires to save his life will lose it; but whoever loses his life for MY sake will find it. Matthew 16:25.

Man can gain the whole world at the cost of his own soul. But what can he give in exchange of his soul (26)? Unless one desires himself and follow Jesus by taking up the cross, he cannot save his life (24).

The soul that sins shall die. Ezek 18:20.

The wickedness of the wicked shall be only upon him, and not on his parents or his children. Every soul will be responsible for its own sins and there cannot be any family member or any representative to bear the iniquity of the soul.

But, I will remember the years of the right hand of the most High. Ps 77:10.

Accepting his infirmity, the Psalmist Asaph remembers and confirms with us that our years are in the right hand of the most High, our Lord. The Lord holds our end with Him, and if He had given the end in advance to every one of us, there will never be happiness in any family. A poet wrote that God gave everything to mankind but kept PEACE with Him, so that man would not forget God. How true! If every soul carries an expiry date, how would the world be? Let us praise Him for the PEACE left with us.

Life and Death

"Behold, I set before you the way of life, and the way of death."

Jer 21:8.

Life and Death

Indeed, you have made my days as handbreadths. Ps 39:5.

The Psalmist tells God that his age is nothing before the Lord, Who made his days as handbreadth. Man heaps up riches and knows not who shall gather them (16), but the hope of the Psalmist is in the Lord (7).

Now my days are swifter than a runner; They flee always; they see no good. Job 9:25.

Like the Psalmist, Job also claims that his days are swifter than a post and the earth is given into the hands of the wicked (24). Despite his righteousness, Job makes his supplication to the Lord (15).

Are not my days a few? Job 10:20

And what is the measure of my days? Ps 39:4.

When Job says that his days are only a few, David pleads with the Lord to let him know his end as well as to give him a mind to count or measure his days. This prayer cannot be answered by our Lord, as it is against His plan.

In whose hands is the life of every living thing, and the breath of all mankind? Job 12:10.

Job answers his three friends and asks them whether they know who has the life of every creature and mankind in His hands, and confirms that the hand of the Lord has (9).

You take away their breath, they die and return to their dust. Ps 104:29.

In the great and wide sea, there are innumerable creeping creatures, both small and great, and our Lord gives them all His breath to live as they would die when He takes away His breath from them at any time.

Lest I sleep the sleep of death. Ps 13:3.

Psalmist David was in deep sorrow and trouble because of his enemies and, in that situation, he thought that the Lord had forgotten him and told Him to lighten his eyes and not to lead him to death, as he has his trust in His mercy and he will sing unto the Lord (Ps 13:6).

The child is not dead, but sleeping. Mark 5:39.

Earlier, the Psalmist referred to the sleep of death but here the Lord says that the child is not dead but sleeping. In the case of Lazarus, He said the same (John 11:11). Therefore, the Lord does not find any difference between the two states of sleeping and death.

Our days on earth are a shadow. Job 8:9.

Job, who earlier told his friend Bildad that his days would flee away like a post, says here that our days (not his days) upon earth are a shadow.

For by me (wisdom) thy days will be multiplied; and years of thy life shall be increased. Pro 9:11.

Wisdom is none other than our Lord Himself, Who multiplies our days and adds years of life as the knowledge of the Holy is understanding (9:10). Also, the fear of the Lord prolongs our life (10:27).

Behold, the eye of the Lord is on those who fear Him…to deliver their soul from death. Ps 33:18-19.

There is a possibility of getting our souls delivered from death if we have fear of the Lord and hope in His mercy. The best advantage to us will be that the eyes of our Lord will be on us.

And you He made alive, who were dead in trespasses and sins. Eph 2:1.

The death specified here is a spiritual death of the state of the natural men who are still living in their sins, alienated from the life of God (4:18 & 19). Even though we were dead earlier in sins, we are saved by the grace of God. Other reference of spiritual death is given in Gen 2:17 as prior warning.

For love is as strong as death. SoS 8:6.

Separation between the lovers is as painful as death, which is referred to here. True love cannot be destroyed even by floods, and its value cannot be compared to the initial substance of our entire house. But the love referred in Cor 13 is meant for Jesus Christ, our Lord and it could be realised if you replace the word 'love' with the name Jesus.

So teach us to number our days, that we may gain a heart of wisdom. Ps 90:12.

Like the Psalmist asked earlier (39:4), here, Moses, the man of God, prays to God to grant him the wisdom, the heart of wisdom (which means heart of God) to number our days. Yet, there is no provision for anyone to know the day of our end.

He who does not have the Son of God does not have life. John 5:12.

He who has the Son of God in him has life, and he who has faith in God has everlasting life (John 6:47) (3:16). Knowing the only true God and His son Jesus Christ who was sent to save us is also the life eternal (John 17:3).

I am the resurrection and the life. He who believes in Me shall never die. John 11:25 & 26.

Here too we see about eternal life as Jesus Christ who is the resurrection and life, and His commandment is life everlasting (12:50).

This year you shall die, because you have taught rebellion against the Lord. Jer 28:16.

God Who has in His hands the days and months, tells Hannaniah, the prophet, that he would die that year as he taught rebellion against the Lord. Hananiah died accordingly, on the seventh month of the same year. Even prophets are not exempted from the punishment of death (Deut 13:5).

ଔଷ

My days are like a shadow that lengthens, and I wither away like grass. Ps 102:11.

The life of our days is like a shadow and it withers away like grass – the Psalmist confirms his knowledge in this truth to the Lord in his prayer.

ଔଷ

Man is like to vanity; his days are as a shadow that passeth away. Ps 144.4.

Man is not worthy of the love of our Lord as his life is vanity and his days are like passing shadow. Happy are those whose God is the Lord (15).

ଔଷ

On his death bed, Alexander summoned his army generals and told them his three final wishes:

#1. Only the best doctors should carry his coffin.

#2. The wealth he had accumulated (money, gold, precious stones) should be scattered along the procession to the cemetery.

#3. His hands should be let loose, so they hang outside the coffin for all to see.

One of his generals, who was surprised by these unusual requests, asked Alexander to explain. He said,

#1. "I want the best doctors to carry my coffin to demonstrate that, in the face of death, even the best doctors in the world have no power to heal."

#2. "I want the road to be covered with my treasure so that everybody sees that material wealth acquired on earth, will stay on earth."

#3. "I want my hands to swing in the wind, so that people understand that we come to this world empty handed and we leave this world empty handed after the most precious treasure of all is exhausted, and that is TIME."

Growth of Death

"They are all gone out of the way." Rom 3:12.

"For the wages of sin is death.

Rom 6:23.

Growth of Death

Your covenant with death will be disannulled and your agreement with hell shall not stand…then you will be trampled down by it. Is 28:18.

Ephraim claimed that they have made (15) a covenant with death that it will not come upon them. But the Lord said to them that their covenant with death shall be disannulled and their agreement with hell shall not stand and the death shall come upon them. No covenant can hold our death.

The wicked man shall die in his iniquity. Ezek 3:18-20.

The onus to warn the wicked and his life is on us—and, if we fail, we become responsible for his blood as the wicked will certainly die in his iniquity.

At evening my wife died. Ezek 24:18.

The rebellions were warned by the Lord that they shall be judged according to their doings. To give them a sign, the Lord told Ezekiel in the morning that He would take away from him his wife. In the evening, his wife died and Ezekiel was made as a sign to them.

꧁

Do I have any pleasure at all that the wicked should die? Ezek 18:23.

Our Lord will not be happy over the death of the wicked. He wants them to repent and turn from all their sins and keep all His statutes, and do what is lawful and right so that they shall surely live and shall not die.

꧁

Therefore turn and live, for I have no pleasure in the death of one who dies, says the Lord God. Ezek 18:32.

The Lord expects the wicked to repent and save their lives from punishment of going to hell, "where their worm dieth not and the fire is not quenched" (Mark 9:44).

꧁

Let us lay aside every weight and the sin…let us run with endurance the race that is set before us. Heb 12:1.

Having been warned again and again, we are expected to repent and be away from all our sins and run our race set before us by considering the numerous witnesses given in the Bible and looking at our Lord Jesus Christ, Who is the author and finisher of our faith.

꧁

All flesh is as grass and all the glory of man as the flower of grass. 1 Pet 1:24.

Whether we are beautiful or not, we take all efforts to make us look presentable and consider our glory as a great one, forgetting the fact that our flesh is just like grass and fallible like flowers. We need to be more concerned about our soul than our bodies (flesh).

ଓ৪ଚ

They will give an account to Him who is ready to judge the living and the dead. 1 Pet 4:5.

The Gospel was preached also to those who already died that they might be judged and hence we should never forget that we are accountable to the Lord in His judgement as we are expected to live according to God in Spirit.

ଓ৪ଚ

If, by any means, I may attain to the resurrection from the dead. Phil 3:11.

Apostle Paul was ever ready to leave this world with the object of desire for fellowship in resurrection power and if we also follow him and press towards the high calling of God in Jesus Christ for taking the prize from Him, we can be sure of our place in heaven.

ଓ৪ଚ

The girl is not dead but sleeping. Matth 9:24.

Even if you are dead, God can give you life and raise you up. But people did not have this faith in Him and they laughed at Him when He said, "The girl is not dead but sleeping." Yet our Lord ignored them and took the child by His hand and she rose up. Faith matters even in death.

ଓ৪ଚ

We should not trust in ourselves but in God, WHO raised the dead. II Cor 1:9.

As explained previously, our God can raise up the dead, and Apostle Paul says that they have trusted the Lord and accordingly they were delivered from the death.

But many who are first will be last, and the last first. Matth 19:30.

The Lord assured His Apostles of places and honour for them in His Kingdom and said to them that anyone who has forsaken anything for His sake shall receive hundred-fold and shall inherit everlasting life, but quoted the possibilities that the publicans and harlots could go into the Kingdom on availing salvation before the Apostles. Matthew 21:31.

Who alone has immortality. 1 Tim 6:16.

Our Lord is the only Potentate, the King of kings, and Lord of lords (15), and He alone has immortality, dwelling in the light that no man can approach unto or seen, nor can see, to Whom be honour and power everlasting.

Anyone who keeps My word, he shall never see death. John 8:51.

Spiritual death is referred here by Jesus, replying to Jews with other reference given in John 11:25, where He said to Martha, "I am the resurrection, and the life, he that believes in Me, though he were dead, yet shall he live!"

To live is Christ and to die is gain. Phil 1:21.

In verse 22, Apostle expresses his confusion but chooses to be in this world for the sake of souls to be saved, despite his interest to be with Christ (23) which he considers better than being here. When we reach such a status of the Apostle, death will not only be a gain but also a joy to us.

Why should you die before your time? Eccl 7:17.

He who fears God does not have to destroy himself, otherwise he may have to die before his time. It is good that you should not be wicked or foolish.

No one has power in the day of death. Eccl 8:8.

Man has no power over his spirit or his day of death. God has appointed bounds that he cannot pass (Job 14:5), so that they that trust in their wealth and boast about themselves will fail on the day of their death. (Ps:49:6).

Then I saw the wicked buried, who had come and be gone from the place of holiness and they were forgotten. Eccl 8:10.

How can the wicked come and be gone from the place of holiness? The hypocrites who appear to be holy in their regular life but leading a wicked life were buried and forgotten.

For the living know that they will die; and the dead know nothing. Eccl 9:5.

The living do not know about their end, their death, and it does not matter to the dead. The preacher says further that there is no remembrance of former things, or of things that are to come with those that shall come later. Everything and everyone is forgotten.

It is appointed for men to die once, but after this the judgement. Heb 9:27.

Death is appointed for everyone and also the judgement after death, as Christ bore our sins already on the cross. When He comes next time, He shall be the Judge and one cannot expect either grace or mercy from Him in His judgement.

଼

The breath of the Almighty given me life. Job 33:4.

God breathed into the nostrils of man the breath of life, says Gen 2:7 and Job understands that the breath of Almighty has given him life, which we too must understand without doubts.

I die daily. 1 Cor 15:31.

For the sake of the Lord, we are killed all the day long, says Romans 8:36, and we are open to spiritual challenges every day and these challenges will never separate us from the love of Christ.

I am forgotten like a dead man. Ps 31:12.

As we saw in Eccl 8:10, the wicked are buried and forgotten, but the Psalmist says that he was also forgotten like a dead man. This is endorsed in Ps 88:5 and 6 too, whereby we are reminded to have the faith of Psalmist to look upon the Lord at every circumstance.

My times are in your hand. Ps 31:15.

Having felt that he was forgotten like a dead man, Psalmist David affirms here his faith that his life is in the hand of our

Lord. Do we have such faith in the Lord?

For, if ye believe not than I am HE, you shall die in your sins. John 8:24.

We are all aware of the wages of sin. We need forgiveness and salvation in order to save us from the wages of sin. In addition we need to believe that Jesus Christ is the son of God who came to save us, failing which we will die in our sins (21).

The number of his months are with thee thou hast appointed his bounds that he cannot pass. Job 14:5.

"Is there not an appointed time to man upon Earth?" asks Job 7:1. To this question, Job himself answers that the Lord has appointed bounds that man cannot pass, as the number of his days and months are with Him. One day, a young boy asked a elderly man, "Sir, which is the best day to pray?" The wise man said, "My son, the best day to pray is the day before you die." The boy was astonished and replied, "Sir, how can I know the day of my death?" The old man answered, "No one knows the day of his/her death. That is why we need to pray everyday."

Therefore let us not sleep, as do others; but let us watch and be sober. 1 Thes 5:6.

Watch therefore; for ye know not what hour your Lord doth come. Matth 24:42.

The Open Choice

> "I have set before you life and death, blessings and
> cursing, therefore choose life, that both
> thou and thy seed may live."
>
> Duet 30:19.

The Open Choice

Life or death was not able to separate Apostle Paul from the love of God, which was in Christ our Lord. Rom 8:38 & 39.

It is important that we should also come to the confidence level of Apostle Paul—that nothing of this world shall be able to separate us from the love of God, which is in Jesus Christ our Lord.

CSƐO

To be carnally minded is death. Rom 8:6.

Apostle Paul confirms the definition of death that any mind related to flesh (13) that anyone who works towards his advantage of the flesh shall (Gal 6:8) reap death but whoever works towards the spiritual advantage shall reap not only everlasting life but also peace.

CSƐO

For the law of the Spirit of life in Christ Jesus has made me free from the law of sin and death. Rom 8:2.

There is a law of the Spirit and a law of sin and death. As the law of Spirit of life is in Jesus Christ our Lord, it saves us from the law of sin and death.

For he that is dead is free from sin. Rom 6:7.

Jesus Christ suffered in His flesh for our sins to get us salvation whereby once we are dead to our sins we are free from our sins through the forgiveness given by our Lord and we become a new creation in Christ.

Have the gates of death been opened unto thee? Have you seen the doors of the shadow of death? Job 38:17.

The chapters 38-41 of Job covered wonderfully the wonders of creations of God. Knowing well about Job's terrible situation, God asked him whether he has experienced the darkness of death and assured him what was declared by Psalmist: "You have lifted me up from the gates of death (Ps 9:13) "for the Lord holds the keys of hell and of death" (Rev 1:18).

He that believeth and is baptised shall be saved; but he that believeth not shall be damned. Mark 16:16.

For it is the power of God unto salvation to everyone that believeth...The just shall live by faith. Rom 1:16 & 17.

Though I walk through the valley of the shadow of death, I will fear no evil. Ps 23:4.

Fearing no evil at the valley of the shadow of death will not be an easy task unless you are very close to the Lord, as was David. Jonah experienced fear of death, as did Hezekiah and Jeremiah. We need to remember that fear is a sin, which is normally used by the devil to influence us to listen to him. None can keep alive his soul (Ps. 22:29). Kingdoms belong to the Lord and He is the ruler of all nations (28) and all the rich and poor who worship the Lord will go to the dust and none of them can keep their soul alive, unless he or she got salvation.

ꕥ

All the increase of thine house shall die in the flower of their age. Sam 2:33.

This was the curse given to Eli by the Lord because of his sons' sins—that there shall not be any old man in his house forever, and all in his house shall die young. Accordingly, Eli's two sons Hophni and Phinehas died young on the same day.

ꕥ

You shall go to your fathers in peace. You shall be buried in a good old age. Gen 15:15.

Contrary to the curse on Eli's family, Abraham was blessed that he shall die in peace at a good old age. Abraham accordingly lived for 175 years and died (25:7 & 8).

ꕥ

These all died in faith. Heb 11:13.

From Abraham to the present generation, many died with their faith that they shall be reaching a city that has permanent foundation and built by God Himself (10).

ꕥ

They shall rise from the dead…but are as the angels in heaven. Mark 12:25.

The dead shall rise from the death and shall be like angels in heaven. In a moment, in the twinkling of an eye, at the last trump…the dead shall be raised incorruptible, (1 Cor 15:52) in glory (43) bearing the image of the heavenly (4O). What an honour for those who die in Christ.

And deliver them who through fear of death were all in their lifetime subject to bondage. Heb 2:15.

God put everything of the world in subjection under the feet of man. Yet he became slave to the world (8) because of sins—hence, he was through fear of death subject to bondage. But Jesus, through His sufferings of death, was crowned with glory and honour, and saved men.

Destroy him that had the power of death, that is, the devil. Heb 2:14.

It was needed for the Lord to take part in flesh and blood, as children are partakers of flesh and blood. He came to the world and, by His sufferings and death on the cross, He destroyed the devil who had the power of death.

There remains therefore a rest to the people of God. Heb 4:9.

A better rest for every believer is created by God. As we have a great high priest, Jesus, the son of God, passed into heavens, let us hold fast to our faith to reach the better rest organised by Him.

Our days on the earth are as a shadow, and there is none abiding. 1 Chr 29:15.

We do not belong to this world and we are strangers and sojourners like our forefathers and, hence, our days on the earth are like just shadows (Also Ps 39:12, Heb 11:13, & 1 Pet 2:11).

The Spirit shall return unto God who gave it. Eccl 12:7.

When man returns to his origin, the dust as cursed by the Lord, the breath given by Him for life shall go back to Him.

The dead shall hear the voice of the Son of God and they that hear shall live. John 5:25.

Verily, verily, says the Lord, he that hears My word and believes that I have sent My son will have everlasting life and shall not come into condemnation, but is passed from death unto life. He says further, "The hour is coming, and now is when the dead shall hear the voice of the Son of God; and all those who hear His voice shall have life. Everyone who sees the Son of God, and believes in Him may have everlasting life and I will raise him at the last day." (John 6:40). Whoever believes the Son of God will have everlasting life and the Lord shall raise them up from dead on the last day (47 & 54). This is the best assurance given to every child of God.

And when they heard of the resurrection of the dead…Acts 17:32.

When the fact remains as stated earlier, the people of Athens were not willing to believe Apostle Paul, who shared these facts with them on death and resurrection. How about you?

⁂

It was expected that one man should die for the people…John 18:14.

Caiaphas, the high priest, prophesied that Jesus should die for that nation and not only for the nation, but also for all children of God that were scattered (11:51 & 52)—since then, they were planning to kill Jesus.

⁂

Knowing that shortly I must put off this my tabernacle, even as our Lord Jesus Christ has shewed me. II Peter 1:14.

Peter, knowing that he would be leaving this world, did not want to neglect his responsibility of reminding people (including us) in order to establish them in truth (12-14).

⁂

For if by one man's offence, death reigned by one… righteousness shall reign in life by one, Jesus Christ…Rom 5:17.

Death was brought into the world by the sin of one man, but there are those who receive the abundance of grace and of the gift of righteousness shall reign in life through Jesus Christ.

⁂

There is no good in them, but for a man to rejoice and to do good in his life…Eccl 3:12

The preacher proclaims that man in his life should rejoice and do only good, which is what is destined and expected by our Lord.

Son, remember that thou in thy lifetime received your good things, but now he is comforted, and you are tormented. Luke 16:25.

Abraham from heaven addressed the rich man that he received in his lifetime on Earth good things but Lazarus received evil things, whereby the rich is tormented and Lazarus is comforted—a wonderful warning for us.

And in those days shall men seek death, and shall not find it. Rev 9:6.

An Angel flying through the midst of heaven said with a loud voice "Woe, woe, woe to the inhabitors of earth" (8:13). At this situation, those whose names are not found in the book of life shall seek death and death shall flee from them.

But that all should come to repentance. II Pet 3:9.

We all know that the coming of the Lord would be any time, but He is still patient in order to have everyone repented. Please, let us remember this and be ready to receive Him any time.

Set thy house in order; for thou shall die, and not live.

II K 20:1.

Hezekiah was informed about his death by Prophet Isaiah but he prayed to God and had his life extended for 15 years more. But this was given to us as a witness to prove the power of God on life as claimed by His word. But this is not open to everyone of this age as we all are closer to His coming.

For here have we no continuing city but we seek one to come. Heb 13:14.

Apostle Paul in Philippians 3:20 said that our citizenship is in heaven, where from we wait upon our Saviour Lord Jesus Christ to come. It is said in Hebrews, for here have we no city, but we seek one to come. For Abraham looked for a city that has foundations made and built by God. (Hebrew. 11:10). As they all desire for a better country, an heavenly one, the Lord has prepared one for them (11:16).

What is your desire? What is your faith? Are you eligible to be part of the city that the Lord prepared for His children? If not, seek for His forgiveness, take His salvation and wait for His call.

He that rejecteth me, and receiveth not my words, hath me that judgeth him; the word that I have spoken, the same shall judge him in the last day. John 12:48.

But I say unto you, It shall be more tolerable for Tyre and Sidon at the day of judgement, than for you. Matthew 11:22.

Be Born Again (Baptism)

> "Except a man be born again, he cannot see the Kingdom of God."
>
> John 3:3

What is Baptism?

The term 'baptism' was derived from the Greek word 'baptizo', which means dipping or immersing into water. According to the Word of God, the Bible, there is only one Baptism as in the case of one Lord and one faith (Eph 4:5).

Apostle Paul in his testimony says that he was told to "arise, and be baptised, and wash away his sins, calling on the name of the Lord." Washing away the sins does not mean as we wash our face or hands or legs—the whole body has to be washed, whereby the whole body has to be immersed into the water symbolically.

When Peter was asked, "What shall we do to repent?" he told them, "Repent, and be baptised, every one of you, in the name of Jesus Christ for the remission of sins and you shall receive the gift of the Holy Spirit." (Acts 22:37-41) Then they gladly received his word and were baptised. There were around 3,000 people who availed baptism. Similarly, when the keeper of the prison that Paul was in realised the need for salvation, the only condition he was given "Believe in the Lord Jesus Christ, and thou shall be saved, and thy house."

The Word of God was shared with him and his family, and they all availed salvation followed by baptism (Acts 16:31–34). The baptism made the entire family rejoice, believing in God.

When Philip preached the things concerning the Kingdom of God and the name of Jesus Christ, both men and women were baptised, and they received the Holy Spirit (Acts 8:12&16). This does not mean that all who are baptised will be anointed simultaneously by Holy Spirit, as they may receive the anointing at a later stage at the appointed time of Lord. In my case as well, I was anointed only after 10 years after the time I got baptised. When Crispus, the Chief ruler of Synagogue, believed in the Lord with all his house, and many of the Corinthians hearing believed, and were baptised (Acts 18:8).

The heart of Lydia was opened when she heard the message of the Lord from Apostle Paul and she and her household were baptised (Acts 16:15).

When all these people of various status have been baptised on hearing the Word of God,

Why Not You?

Biblical Baptisms

Baptism in Christ: When we become the children of Jesus Christ by faith, we are baptised into Him and wear Him on us, that we produce His character in us, and become one in Jesus Christ (God 3:26–28).

Baptism of John (Luke 20:4): John was called John the Baptist, and, invariably, he was professionally labelled as Baptist (John 1:26) as he gave baptism to many and also to

Jesus. He was called to give water Baptism (John 1:33).

Baptism of Spirit: Jesus Christ was meant to give baptism with Holy Spirit (John 1:33). The Baptist also said, "A man can receive nothing, except it be given to him from heaven, when his disciples told him about Jesus giving baptism." Paul confirmed in 1 Cor 10:2 that all our forefathers were baptised unto Moses in the cloud.

Baptism of Paul: Apostle Paul baptised none other than Crispus, Gaius and Stephen's family, in the name of Jesus Christ. Yet, he said he was not sent by Christ to baptise, but to preach the Gospel, not with the wisdom of words, lest the Cross of Christ should be made of no effect (1 Cor 1:14-17).

By tradition, many practice 'child baptism' and I wonder whether to bring that into this heading, as the practice concerned is not Biblical. Baptism demands repentance, forgiveness, salvation and anointing. As such, why does a child need repentance? Jesus Christ referred to children and asked people to be like children to enter the Kingdom of God, as children are sinless (Mark 10:15). The practice of naming the child can be called either 'Christening' (cultural) or 'Dedication' to the Lord as we see in the Word of God. Also, what do children know about faith and salvation (Mark 16:16)? Therefore, one has to understand that 'Child Baptism' is not Biblical. Jesus did not take baptism when he was a child (Luke 2:22-24). Let us follow the examples He showed us.

Who needs "Baptism"?

Whether we be Jews or gentiles, whether we be bonded or free, everyone needs baptism—by one Spirit, we could be baptised into one body (1 Cor 12:13). The Eanuch of great authority under Queen of the Ethiopians came to worship and, while he was returning in his chariot, he was reading about the Prophet Isaiah in scripture but did not understand much. He was given the message of salvation by Philip, and then was saved and baptised (Acts 8:36-38). Similarly, when gentiles were anointed by the Holy Spirit, Peter asked, "Can any man forbid that these should not be baptised?" (Acts 10:44-48). Therefore whether you are regular in reading the scripture or prayer or attending worships, you need baptism to get the heavenly knowledge to understand the scriptures better.

The Samarias heard the preaching of Philip on the Kingdom of God and Jesus Christ and both men and women were baptised (Acts 8:12), which confirms that no gender is exempted from the requirement. Corinthians were also baptised (Acts 18:8). However, when John the Baptist saw the Pharisees and Sadducees come to him to get baptised, he addressed them as a generation of vipers for he knew about their inner mind (Matth 3:6 &7).

And all the people that heard him and the publicans justified God on being baptised, but the Pharisees and lawyers rejected the council of God against themselves (Luke 7:29-30).

How About You?

Why is Baptism Necessary?

Jesus said, "Verily, verily, I say into thee, except a man be born of water and of the Spirit, he cannot enter into the Kingdom of God" (John 3:5).

When the Philippian jailor asked Apostle Paul, "What must I do to be saved?", he was told to believe on the Lord Jesus Christ, "and thou shall be saved, and thy house." Consequently the entire family was baptised (Acts 16:30-34).

These two verses emphasis on the necessity for every believer to be baptised, if only they have faith in Lord Jesus Christ.

Only baptism could bury the sinful past of a person, as he or she on baptism becomes dead to their sins wherein he/she is risen with Him through the faith of the operation of God, Who raised the baptised person from the dead (Col 2:12).

For the flesh lusteth against the Spirit and the Spirit against the flesh, and these are contrary to one to another—so that one cannot do the things that one could (Gal 5:17), whereby one needs to have the support of the Holy Spirit which could be availed only through baptism. When a believer walks in the Spirit (V16), he/she cannot fulfill the lust of the flesh.

Eligibility to Take Baptism

You are absolutely eligible to take baptism immediately if you have faith in our Lord and His Kingdom.

And all flesh shall see the salvation of God says Luke 3:6, but in verse 7, John calls the multitude "O generation of vipers", which means John was able to see the hearts of the multitude and found them unclean—whereby we can understand that only the clean-hearted are eligible to get baptised, based on their faith.

Then, they that gladly received His word were baptised (Acts 2:41) after repentance (38), which means one has to accept the Word of God gladly, without any doubt, in order to be eligible to get baptised.

When they believed Philip preaching the things concerning the Kingdom of God and the name of Jesus Christ, they were baptised (Acts 8:12). Therefore it is an important criteria to have belief and faith in the name of our Lord Jesus Christ and also in His Kingdom, and the Word that God sent unto the children of Israel, preaching peace by Jesus Christ, which was published throughout all Judea and began from Galilee, after the baptism which John preached (Acts 10:36–37).

Hence, the Word on baptism is shared with you so that you will not delay your decision.

The Benefits of Baptism

Salvation is available through baptism after getting forgiveness of sins. He that believeth and is baptised shall be saved; but he that believeth not shall be damned (Mark 16:16).

And all the people that heard him and the publicans, justified God being baptised with the baptism of John (Luke 7:29). But the Pharisees and lawyers rejected the counsel of God against themselves, being not baptised of him (30). Thus Mark 16:16 became applicable to them.

Repent and be baptised every one of you in the name of Jesus Christ for the remission of sins, and ye shall receive the gift of Holy Spirit (Acts 2:38) said Peter. What can be a better gift than the Holy Spirit?

For if, when we were enemies, we were reconciled to God by the death of His Son, much more, being reconciled, we shall be saved by His life (Romans 5:10).

Therefore, we are buried with Him by baptism into death; that like as Christ was raised up from the dead by the glory of the Father, even so we also should walk in newness of life (Rom 6:4). At this stage, we know that for he that is dead is freed from sin (7).

We get special honour from the co-believers as Apostle Paul got from Lydia soon after she and her family were baptised (Acts 16:15).

Therefore if any man be in Christ, he is a new creature; old things are passed away: behold all things are became new (II Cor 5:17). What a privilege to become new in the sight of our Lord! In addition to this we will be given the ministry of reconciliation (II Cor 5:18).

For by grace are ye saved through faith; and that not of yourselves; it is the gift of God (Ept 2:8). The salvation has been gained through faith by His grace, which is another gift of God.

When Christ, Who is our life, shall appear, then shall ye also appear with Him in glory (Col 3:4).

What More Do You Need?

Eligibility to Give Baptism

Although it is simple and easy to take baptism with the faith in our Lord, it is very important that you need to be mindful of who gives you baptism, as I hear that many give baptism without having proper righteousness and holiness.

John the Baptist gave baptism and he was commanded by our Lord that are born of woman there is not a prophet than John the Baptist (Luke 7:28). Yet, he was not only humble but also holy to declare that He that cometh after him is mightier than him, Whose shoes he is not worthy to bear and He shall baptise with the Holy Spirit with fire (Matth 3:11). Therefore, anyone who gives baptism should be humble and holy and God-centered and not self-centered.

One has to realise the status of John the Bapist that Jesus Himself took baptism from him when the Holy Spirit descended and remained on Jesus (John 1:32). One has to give baptism only in the name of the Lord Jesus Christ. When Peter was preaching, the Holy Spirit fell on everyone who heard the word and they all started speaking in tongues (Acts 10:44). Subsequently they were all baptised. This confirms that the presence of Holy Spirit will fall on the baptised if the person giving baptism has the qualities of a saint.

When Apostle Paul came to Ephesus, he met a few disciples who were baptised by Apollo, the Jew—an eloquent man and mighty in the scriptures. Paul asked these disciples, "Have you received the Holy Spirit since ye believed?" But, to his surprise, they replied that they have not so much as heard whether there be any Holy Spirit. Consequently, Paul laid his hands upon them and they spoke in tongues and prophesied (Acts 19:6).

In my personal experience, I got anointed only after 10 years of my baptism. My spiritual father was very keen to have me baptised once again by a particular pastor. But, my brother in Christ, the pastor, was not willing to oblige. Yet, within a short span, in one evening, the Spirit of the Lord fell upon me—which brought several spiritual blessings since then.

Look upon the Lord for His guidance in choosing the person of holiness who could give you baptism in the name of our Lord Jesus Christ.

What Happens Post–Baptism

Take My yoke upon you, and learn of me, for I am meek and lonely in heart; and you shall find rest unto your souls. For my yoke is easy and burden is light (Matth 11:29 & 30). Our Lord who assured rest to us in the previous verse (28), now expects us to take His yoke as this will be a pleasant experience of winning over temptation.

Jesus took baptism when he was 30, and after that was taken into wilderness for 40 days to be tempted by Satan. When Jesus Himself was put through such temptation, how would we be exempted? (Mark 1:13 & Luke 4:2-13). For every temptation, Jesus said, "It is written", and won the temptation. Whatever doubts you have either about baptism or anything else, you can refer to the Word of God—which has an answer for everything as said in Is 34:16. The Bible is a talking resource of our Lord and you can make use of it at every situation.

And the World passeth away and the lust thereof; but he that doeth the will of God abideth for ever (1 John 2:17). Your taking baptism is the will of God in your life and once you obey, you shall abide with Him forever.

Jesus Christ had another baptism which you and I cannot participate in, as it was the CROSS in which He was crucified towards the WAGES of our sins to give us salvation (Luke 12:50). There shall be peace ruling your heart and you need to be grateful to God for you are also given an opportunity to abide with Him through baptism. And let the peace of God rule in your hearts, to which also you are called in one body; and be ye thankful (Col 3:15). The peace, which is available nowhere in the world will belong to you.

AND NOW WHY TARRIEST THOU? ARISE AND BE BAPTISED, AND WASH AWAY THY SINS, CALLING ON THE NAME OF THE LORD. FOR THOU SHALL BE HIS UNTO ALL MEN OF WHAT THOU HAST SEEN AND HEARD. Acts 22: 16 & 15

The Commission

ALL POWER IS GIVEN UNTO ME IN HEAVEN AND EARTH. GO YE THEREFORE, AND TEACH ALL NATIONS, BAPTISING THEM IN THE NAME OF THE FATHER, AND OF THE SON AND OF THE HOLY GHOST: TEACHING THEM TO OBSERVE ALL THINGS WHATSOEVER I HAVE COMMANDED YOU: AND, LO. I AM WITH YOU ALWAYS, EVEN UNTO THE END OF THE WORLD. AMEN

JESUS CHRIST

MATTHEW 28:18-20

The Inheritance

THEN SHALL THE KING SAY UNTO THEM ON HIS RIGHT HAND,

COME, YE BLESSED OF MY FATHER, INHERIT THE KINGDOM PREPARED FOR YOU FROM THE FOUNDATION OF THE WORLD.

MATTHEW 25:34

Our Hope

> "Which is Christ in you, the hope of glory."
>
> Col 1:27.

Our Hope

We have a building of God, an house not made with hands, eternal in the heaven. II Cor 5:1.

Can we think or visualise a house built without the use of hands? Our Lord assures His children that if their earthly houses are dissolved here, there will be a house built by God Himself in heaven.

Wherefore I praised the dead who are already dead more than the living who are yet alive. Eccl 4:2.

Having seen the suppressions and tears of the suppressed, who had no one to comfort them, King Solomon the Preacher says that the dead are blessed than those living with tears under the sun. He further appreciates that those who were not born were more blessed. But the Lord says that He will set them in safety. Ps 11:5.

And you shall know that I am the Lord, when I have opened your graves. Ezek 37:13.

Restoration of Israel (the dry bones) is well explained in this chapter. The graves are their nations and by bringing them out of their graves, the Lord shall put His spirit in them and they shall live (14).

And I shall put my spirit in you and ye shall live…Ezek 37:14.

On putting His spirit in them, the Lord shall place them in their own land so that they will know and accept that the Lord has spoken it and performed it.

In 1923, nine of the wealthiest people in the world met at Chicago's Edge Water Beach Hotel.

Their combined wealth, it is estimated, exceeded the wealth of the United States government at that time. These men certainly knew how to make a living and accumulate wealth. Attending the meeting were the following men:

1. The President of the largest steel company
2. The President of the largest utility company
3. The President of the largest gas company
4. The President of the New York Stock Exchange
5. The President of the Bank of International Settlements
6. The greatest wheat speculator
7. The greatest bear on Wall Street
8. The head of the world's greatest monopoly, and
9. A member of President Harding's cabinet.

That's a pretty impressive line-up of people by anyone's yardstick. Yet, 25 years later, where were those nine industrial giants? Let us examine what happened to them 25 years later:

1. The President of the then largest steel company (Bethlehem Steel Corp), Charles M. Schwab, lived on borrowed capital for five years before he died bankrupt.
2. The President of the then largest gas company, Howard Hubson, went insane.
3. One of the greatest commodity traders (wheat speculator), Arthur Cutten, died an insolvent.
4. The then President of the New York Stock Exchange, Richard Whitney, was sent to jail.
5. The member of the American President's Cabinet (the member of President Harding's cabinet), Albert Fall, was pardoned from jail, just to be able to go home and die in peace.
6. The greatest 'bear' on Wall Street, Jesse Livermore, committed suicide.
7. The President of the then world's greatest monopoly, Ivar Krueger, committed suicide.
8. The President of the Bank of International Settlement, Leon I Fraser, committed Suicide.
9. The President of the largest utility company, Samuel lnsull, died penniless.

What they all forgot was how to 'make' life while they were busy making money. Money in itself is not evil—it provides food for the hungry, medicine for the sick and clothes for the needy. Money is only a medium of exchange.

He that loveth silver shall not be satisfied with silver; nor he that loveth abundance with increase; this is also vanity. Riches kept for the owners thereof to their hurt. As he came forth of his mother's womb, naked shall he return to go as he came, and shall take nothing of his labour, which he may carry away in his hand. Eccl 5:10, 13 & 15.

The righteous has hope in his death. Pro 14:32.

The Lord certified Job as a perfect and upright man and in Job 13:15, he says "Though He slay me, yet I will trust in Him." This is applicable to the righteous who have great faith in the Lord, and they die in peace with the hope of going to the Lord.

Having a desire to depart and to be with Christ, which is far better. Phil 1:23.

This statement of Apostle Paul endorses what was said by Job and Solomon. The separation from this world through death will take us to be with the Lord. Anyone who comes to this faith in the name of our Lord will never be afraid of death but will desire it at the time appointed by Him.

I have finished my course. I have kept the faith II Tim 4:7.

Apostle Paul was ever ready to go to the Lord, as he finished his responsibilities entrusted with him by God and he was confident of getting the 'Crown of righteousness' from the Lord Himself. What is our situation and the status of our race?

The time of the dead, that they should be judged. Rev 11:18.

In the second coming of our Lord, every one will be judged as given in Matth 25:31-46. Appropriate reward is assured to His servants, the prophets, the saints, and to all those who feared His name whether they are small or great. Let us get ready and be prepared to receive the reward.

ഌ

And they overcame him by the blood of the Lamb…they loved not their lives unto the death. Rev 12:11.

Only those who were willing to die/become martyrs for the sake of the Lord, and challenged the devil by the blood of the lamb and their testimony, will be victorious.

ഌ

Blessed are the dead, who die in the Lord from henceforth… Rev 14:13. Precious in the sight of the Lord is the death of His saints. Ps 116:15.

The saints are not exempted from death but their death shall be precious in the sight of the Lord and the Spirit of the Lord confirms that those who die in the Lord shall rest from their labour and all their good deeds would follow them. What a blessing!

ഌ

Shall have their part in the lake which burns with fire and brimstone, which is the SECOND DEATH. Rev 21:8.

While the reward would be given to those who feared the Lord, all sinners shall be put into the lake of fire, which would be the second death.

ഌ

The dead shall live together with my dead body shall they arise. Is 26:19.

The Earth shall cast out the dead and as claimed in Daniel 12:2, "And many of them that sleep in the dust of the earth shall awake, some to shame and everlasting contempt." God has given His children everlasting life, which is in His son. 1 John 5:11.

For the Lord Himself shall descend from heaven with a shout, with a voice of the archangel, and with the trump of God. 1 Thes 4:16.

Those who believed that Jesus died and rose again shall join the Lord, when He comes down from heaven with a shout and voice of the archangel and the trump of God. Those who died in Christ shall rise first, and then the living will meet Him in the air.

Meet the Lord in the air and so shall we ever be with the Lord…1 Thes 4:17.

The wonderful joy is that we shall ever be with the Lord, after meeting Him in the air caught up together in the clouds. What a blessed privilege!

And shall come forth; they that have done good, unto the resurrection of life and they that have done evil unto the resurrection of damnation. John 5:29.

The son of man has the authority to execute judgement, and the end has been conveyed in the Gospel itself to everyone with an opportunity to realise and understand what is given in Revelation.

For whether we…die, we die unto the Lord. Rom 14:8.

None of us should either live or die for ourselves and we will have to live and die for our Lord as claimed by Apostle

Paul: "I am crucified with Christ, nevertheless, I live; and yet not I, but Christ lives in me; and the life which I live now in the flesh I live by the faith of the Son of God, Who loved me and gone Himself for me." Gal 2:20.

ଓଃ୧୦

I will raise him up at the last day. John 6:54.

Partaking in the communion of our Lord in order to remember what He had done for everyone—died for our sins—is organised by our Lord, and whoever eats His flesh and drinks His blood in remembrance will have eternal life and He will raise them up at the last day.

ଓଃ୧୦

For since by man came death, by man came the resurrection of the dead. 1 Cor 15:21.

Having risen from the dead, Christ became the first fruit of the dead since death came by one man; resurrection also came by Christ Who made everyone alive.

ଓଃ୧୦

It is sown in corruption, it is raised in incorruption. 1 Cor 15:42.

Every star differs from one another in glory. Similarly, the resurrection of the dead, those who were sown in corruption raised in incorruption. It is sown in dishonor and it is raised in glory.

ଓଃ୧୦

It is sown in dishonor; it is raised in glory. 1 Cor 15:43.

For our citizenship is in heaven, from where also we look

for the Saviour the Lord Jesus Christ—Who shall change our vile body, that it may be fashioned like unto His glorious body (Phil 3:20, 21).

Then shall be brought to pass the saying that is written, "Death is swallowed up in victory. 1 Cor 15:54.

The Lord shall swallow up death in victory and the Lord God will wipe away tears from all faces, Is 25:8. Accordingly, death was swallowed up in victory by Jesus on the Cross.

Then shall you also appear with Him in glory. Col 3:4.

When Christ, Who is our life, shall appear, we will also appear with Him in glory, which is the believer's union with Christ forever.

Surely I come quickly, Amen. Even so, come Lord Jesus. Rev 22:20.

You might have heard several times that the Lord shall be coming soon. Yet, the Lord Himself is telling you now, "Surely I come quickly", and let us all say together "Amen. Even so come Lord Jesus."

And death and hell were cast into the lake of fire. This is the second death. Rev 20:14.

Finally the book of life was opened, and those whose names were not found in the book were cast into the lake of fire. And also the death and hades, which was the second death.

Looking forward hasting towards the coming of the day

of God, wherein the heavens being on fire shall be dissolved, and the elements shall melt with fervent heat! Nevertheless we, according to His promise, look for new heavens and a new earth, wherein dwells righteousness. Wherefore, beloved seeing that you look for such things, be diligent that you may be found of Him in peace, without spot and blameless. II Peter 3:12-14.

As we are aware of Who holds our future, let us apply our hope of future into our present and be cheerful. The future has its effect on the present.

George Macdonald.

Multitudes, multitudes in the valley of decision, for the day of the Lord is near in the valley of the decision. Joel 3:14.

Wherefore we receiving a Kingdom which cannot be moved, let us have grace, whereby, we may serve God acceptably with reverence and godly fear. Heb 12:28.

Holiness is the greatest power one can have to conquer the greatest enemy, the power of death. When we die with holiness, we are going to entrust our spirit and not our body—into the hands of God, like Jesus Christ and Apostle Stephen.

Courtesy: Morning Manna

But I say unto you, It shall be more tolerable for the land of Sodom in the day of judgement, than for you. Matthew 11:24.

I was shocked, confused, bewildered,

As I entered Heaven's door,

Not by the beauty of it all,

Nor the lights or its decor.

But it was the folks in Heaven,
Who made me sputter and gasp,
The thieves, the liars, the sinners,
The alcoholics and the trash.

There stood the kid from seventh grade,
Who swiped my lunch money twice.
Next to him was my old neighbor,
Who never said anything nice.

Bob, who I always thought,
Was rotting away in hell,
Was sitting pretty on cloud nine,
Looking incredibly well.

I nudged Jesus, 'What's the deal?
I would love to hear Your take,
How'd all these sinners get up here?
God must've made a mistake.

'And why's everyone so quiet?
So somber? give me a clue.'
'Hush, child,' He said, 'They're all in shock.
NO ONE THOUGHT THEY WOULD BE SEEING YOU!'

David J. Nixon

Our Home Eternal

"And no man hath ascended up to heaven but He that came down from heaven, even the Son of man which is in heaven."

John 3:13.

"I go to prepare a place for you…I will come again and receive you to Myself, that when I am, there you may be also."

John 14:2&3.

The Holy City, New Jerusalem, Our Home Eternal

Father's house are many mansions…I go to prepare a place for you. John 14:2.

Although there are many mansions available in our Father's house, Jesus has guaranteed us an exclusive one for everyone. Our citizenship is in heaven. Phil 3:20.

❧

There is laid up for me a crown of righteousness, which the Lord, the righteous judge, shall give me that day. II Tim 4:8.

There is not only an exclusive mansion for us but also a 'Crown of Righteousness' which shall be presented to us by the Lord Himself.

They which are written in the Lamb's book of life only will enter into it. Rev 21:27.

These privileges are given only to those whose names are available in the Lamb's book of life. Flesh and blood cannot inherit the Kingdom of God. 1 Cor 15:50.

To an inheritance, incorruptible, and undefiled, and that fadeth not away, reserved in heaven for you. I Pet 1:4.

For those who are born again (John 3:3), an everlasting inheritance is kept reserved in the Kingdom of God.

How hardly shall they that have riches enter into the Kingdom of God. Mark 10:23.

It is easier for a camel to go through the eye of a needle than for a rich man to enter into the Kingdom of God, said Jesus (25) but it will be still possible for the rich and not for those who trust in their riches (24).

For the hope, which is laid up for you in heaven. Col 1:5.

Based on our faith in Jesus Christ and the love towards the saints, the hope stated in the Word of God has been laid up for you in heaven.

When shall I come and appear before God?. Ps 42:2.

Knowing the wonders of heaven the Psalmist declared, "As the hart panteth after the water brooks, so panteth my soul after God and my soul thirsteth for God, the living God; when shall I come and appear before Him."

ꙮ

To him that overcomes will I give…a white stone, and in the stone, a new name written, which no man knows saving he who receives it. Rev 2:17.

To those who overcome…He will write upon them the name of His God and the name of the City of His God, which is new Jerusalem…He will write upon him His new name. Rev 3:12.

ꙮ

You shall make me full of joy with thy countenance. Acts 2:28.

You shall be filled with joy in His presence, where is fullness of joy; and there are pleasures for evermore at His right hand. Ps 16:11.

ꙮ

He that sitteth on the throne shall dwell among them. Rev 7:15.

There shall be no more hunger or thirst, and there will not be Sun for light and heat, for the Lamb of God who will be in the midst of the throne would feed them and shall lead them unto living fountains of waters.

ꙮ

I am Alpha and Omega, the beginning and the ending, says the Lord, which is, which was and which is to come, the Almighty. Rev 1:8.

Alpha is the first letter and Omega is the last letter of the Greek language, which represents here that He is the

Almighty and everything. It has been stated again and again in 1:11 & 21:6.

I am He that liveth, and was dead, and behold, I am alive for evermore, Amen. Rev 1:18.

Most of us identify the face of our Lord by the picture that was crafted by someone (human) and even the poses have been kept changing according to the views of the modern mind and countries. Even Moses hid his face as he was afraid to look upon God. Ex 3:6. Of course the disciples have seen Jesus Christ and not the Father. Similarly, Jesus Christ was seen by His beloved disciple Apostle John in the vision at Patmos.

Apostle John was in the Spirit on the Lords' day (Sabbath) and heard behind him a great voice as of a trumpet (1:10), saying, "I am Aplha and Omega, the first and the last."

On having heard the voice, John was trying to turn and see the person to whom the voice belonged to. He saw seven golden candlesticks (lampstands) and in the midst of those candlesticks, he saw the One who looked like the Son man—Jesus Christ. He was clothed with a long garment down to the foot and girt about the paps with a golden girdle. His head and hairs were like white wool as white as snow and His eyes were as a flame of Fire. And His feet like unto fine brass, as if they burnt in a furnace, and His voice as the sound of many waters. And He had in His right hand seven stars; and out of His mouth went a sharp two-edged sword; and His countenance was as the sun shines in his strength. And when the Apostle saw Him, he fell at His feet as dead. And He had His right hand upon him and said, Fear not. I am He that lives and was dead; and behold I am alive for evermore. Amen. 1:12-18.

The mystery of the seven stars which seen in His right hand, and the seven golden lampstands—the seven stars are the angels of the seven churches; and the seven lampstands are the seven churches. 1:20.

Can any of our modern technologies describe how our Lord was seen in vision by John? Divine and magnificent features! Daniel also saw in his visions the coming of the Son of man in glory. "I beheld till the thrones were cast down and the Ancient of days did sit, Whose garment was white as snow and the hair of His head like the pure wool; His throne was like the fiery flame and his wheels as burning fire." Dan 7:9.

"Behold, one like the Son of man came with the clouds of heaven, came to the ancient of days, and they brought Him near before Him." Dan 7:13.

"The Lord's throne is in heaven. His eyes behold, His eyelids try the children of men," says the Psalmist 11:4.

But ye are come unto mount Sion, and unto the city of the living God, the heavenly Jerusalem, and to an innumerable company of angels. To the general assembly and the church of the first born, which are written in heaven, and to God, the judge of all, and to the spirits of just men made perfect. And to Jesus the mediator of the new covenant, and to the blood of sprinkling, that speaketh better things than that of Abel." Heb 12:22-24.

Holy Jerusalem, Our Eternal Home

And he carried me away in the spirit to a great and high mountain and shewed me the great city, the holy Jerusalem.

Having the glory of God and her light was like unto a stone most precious, even like a jasper stone, clear as crystal and has a wall, great and high that had twelve gates and at the gates twelve angels, and names written thereon, which are the names of the twelve tribes of children of Israel. On the east three gates; on the north three gates, on the south three gates and on the west three gates.

And the wall of the city had twelve foundations and in them the names of twelve Apostles of the Lamb…

And the building of the wall of it was of jasper and the city was pure gold, like unto clear glass. And the foundations of the wall of the city were garnished with all manner of precious stones. The first foundation was jasper, the second, sapphire, the third, a chalcedony, the fourth an emerald, the fifth, sardonyx, the sixth sardias, the seventh chrysolyte, the eighth, beryl, the ninth a topaz, the tenth, a chrysoprasus; the eleventh, a jascinth, the twelfth, an amethyst. And the twelve gates were twelve pearls; every several gate was of one pearl; and the street of the city was pure gold, as it were transparent glass. And…for the Lord God Almighty and the Lamb are the temple of it.

And the city had no need of the sun, neither of the moon, to shine in it, for the glory of God did lighten it and the Lamb is the light thereof…And the gates of it shall not be shut at all by day for there shall be no night there. Rev 21:10-25.

In the midst of the street of it, and on either side of the river, the water of life, was there the tree of life, which bare twelve manner of fruits and yielded her fruit every month; and the leaves of the tree were for healing of the nations.

The throne of God and of the Lamb shall be in it...And they shall see His face. Rev 22:2-4.

Oh what a day that will be,
When my Jesus I shall see.
When I look upon His face,
The One Who saved me by His grace.
And when He takes me by the hand,
Leads me to the Promised Land,
What a day, glorious day that will be.
(Author unknown)

WELCOME ON BOARD

My Testimony

Chapters 38 to 41 of Job explain that Job was asked question after question by our Lord and Job just shut his mouth with his hand without answering them until God told him to answer. I can now from my experience refer to the verse 17 of chapter 38, "Have the gates of death been opened unto thee? Or hast thou seen the doors of the shadow of death?" and say, "Yes, Lord, I have been there but you brought me back safely by your grace and mercy."

On 21st July, at 3 am, I was admitted at Apollo Hospital at their Emergency Unit. Later that morning, I underwent angioplasty by the most experienced and popular Christian cardiologist. The entire procedure was successful and I was in the CCU at 9 am, and was told that they would discharge me the next day. At noon, a doctor who came to check up on me noticed blood oozing from the punctured spot of my body. I was not aware of it for more than two hours as I was under local anesthesia. I also then noticed that the bandage, my dress and the sheet were soaked with blood. Within a few minutes, the system at my bed raised alarms while I was choking. Everything looked dark, my body was heavy and I had the feeling that a few people were stepping on my chest. My pulse, blood pressure and heart rate were very low and I became disoriented and delirious.

A team of doctors rushed around my bed and tried their best to help me. My throat and mouth went dry. I was at the gateway of death, experiencing the shadow of death, valley of death and darkness of death but I forgot totally what I had heard, told, and read thousands and thousands of times the claim of the Psalmist: "Yea, though I walk through the valley of the shadow of death, I will fear no evil" as well what I have preached about "fear", as a sin. I was filled with fear and nothing but fear. At that moment, I saw the face of my wife on the roof and thought, "it was finished." Then something, prompted me to praise the Lord with 'sthothirams' (Praise the Lord) and after making three sthothirams I started speaking in tongues. Thereafter, I did not know much about what happened except that I was moved to a larger room and connected to life-saving machines and oxygen. After five hours of the doctors' attention, I was brought back to normalcy by God's grace and mercy. With the help of sedation, I slept for 30 minutes and then woke up and saw my wife (who did not know anything about what happened to me inside CCU) and felt better.

As claimed by Prophet Jeremiah and the Psalmist, I join them in saying "Lord, thou has pleaded the causes of my soul; thou has redeemed my life. Lam. 3:58" and "Oh Lord thou has brought up my soul from the grave, thou has kept me alive Ps. 30:3." After experiencing other related complications, I was discharged after nine days and I have no reason to know why God allowed this experience but I wait for His time to know the purpose of it. While I was discharged, I was advised complete bed rest and, during this time I was able to spend around six hours every day with the Word of God, which helped me to complete my manuscript on Eternal Joy in Eternity.

Please join me in praising our Lord for the precious blood of Jesus Christ, which is still fresh and powerful that brought me out of an end to a new beginning.

The Author

This publication is sponsored by:

Church
Planters Council - India
★ ONE FAMILY ★ ONE CHURCH ★ ONE VILLAGE

A-3, I Floor, Gems Court, 14, Khader Nawaz Khan Road
Nungambakkam, Chennai – 600 006
Tel: 044-2833 0600, 2833 0700
Email: planting@churchplanterscouncil.org
www.churchplanterscouncil.org